one whole day

WOLVES

BY JIM ARNOSKY

NATIONAL GEOGRAPHIC SOCIETY

Washington, D.C.

It was a cold November morning.
Snowflakes sifted down
through leafless trees.
A family of timber wolves
padded through the forest…

...their big paws crunching brittle leaves.

A big male led
his mate and
three younger
wolves—
a yearling
female and
her brothers.

The lead wolf watched
the forest warily.

He was cautious,
protective of the others.

All morning long, the wolf pack tracked hunting grouse

or snowshoe hare to eat.

At noontime, they searched for mice
holed up in a boulder pile
or hiding under leaves.

They sniffed and pawed and dug.

They growled and whined and howled
the afternoon away.

Then all at once they took off racing neck and neck,

moving like one
big wolfy shadow
in the dimming
light of day.

Running ahead of the pack,
the lead wolf found a small stream pool
and drank in quiet solitude.

When the other wolves arrived,
they splashed right in,
crowding the small pool.
Then they crossed the stream
together and continued
on their way.

They climbed a snowy hillside
to the very top
and bedded down—

wild wolves falling fast asleep,
ending one wild day.

To create his paintings, Jim Arnosky used an acrylic wash with pencil.

The text type used in this book is set in Veljovic Book.
The title type is set in ITC Cancione, altered by the designer.

Book design by Sharon Davis Thorpe, Panache Designs.

Library of Congress Cataloging-in-Publication Data
available on request.

ISBN: 0-7922-7146-7

Printed in Mexico

The world's largest nonprofit scientific and educational organization, the National Geographic Society was founded in 1888 "for the increase and diffusion of geographic knowledge." Since then it has supported scientific exploration and spread information to its more than eight million members worldwide. The National Geographic Society educates and inspires millions every day through magazines, books, television programs, videos, maps and atlases, research grants, the National Geographic Bee, teacher workshops, and innovative classroom materials. The Society is supported through membership dues, charitable donations, and income from the sale of its educational products. Members receive NATIONAL GEOGRAPHIC magazine—the Society's official journal—discounts on Society products and other benefits.
For more information about the National Geographic Society, its educational programs and publications, and ways to support its work, please call 1-800-NGS-LINE (647-5463) or write to the following address:

NATIONAL GEOGRAPHIC SOCIETY
1145 17th Street N.W.
Washington, D.C. 20036-4688
U.S.A.

Visit the Society's Web site at www.nationalgeographic.com

For Eddie